## About the Author

Born of humble beginnings, David, now fifty-four, is an accomplished Fund Manager. He is married and father to three adult children.

# The Forever Field

# David Pace

# The Forever Field

Olympia Publishers
*London*

**www.olympiapublishers.com**
OLYMPIA PAPERBACK EDITION

**Copyright © David Pace 2023**

The right of David Pace to be identified as author of
this work has been asserted in accordance with sections 77 and 78 of
the Copyright, Designs and Patents Act 1988.

A CIP catalogue record for this title is
available from the British Library.

ISBN: 978-1-80439-653-7

This is a work of fiction.
Names, characters, places and incidents originate from the writer's
imagination. Any resemblance to actual persons, living or dead, is
purely coincidental.

First Published in 2023

Olympia Publishers
Tallis House
2 Tallis Street
London
EC4Y 0AB

Printed in Great Britain

# Dedication

To my mother-who suffered so I wouldn't have to.

# Acknowledgements

Thank you to those that encouraged my humble scribing. Thank you to my wife Claudia and children Marcus, Carla and Catia without who's love and support this would never have happened.

# Forward

For Salvatore and Pierre Luigi who guided me toward fiction
and all of it's wonderment.

My essays lie there scattered on the floor, for fill their need just
by being there – David Bowie

Agonise over every word as if your last
Each metaphor your parting bemuse
Every phrase your endmost pondering – David Pace

# Preface

It is me on every page
The love, the struggle, the pain
I'm there in obscurity and at times indisputably
I'm there in sunlight, in complete darkness – lurking in shadows
Every word is etched of my blood – at times of my jugular at
others stymied by coagulation
On every page lie my entrails, extracted and rearranged for your
bemuse

# Before the Metaphor

Before the metaphor;
A thought was simply a thought,
An emotion purely an emotion – a word something unequivocal.
Her smile was 'just' beautiful.
His heart 'just' fluttered.
Their love and adoration for each other – no more, no less
convoluted than that.

The universe intermittently offers us moments of stillness,
Embracing or neglecting them is the difference between peace
and destruction.
Be peaceful x

# Forgone Farewell

When time bares down on you
And you summon me to your side
Your malfeasance in closing?
Finally the stench of vulnerability, the hideousness of fear
hovers over you, not I

You had me endure this hell
This forsaken edifice of your construct
The same affliction you now desire to abandon
Find another to relieve your encumbrance for I pledged in good
faith; I would forever harbour he from my youth from your evil

And as you, of "honourable" tidings, draw your final breath
may that young boy with a stutter – downtrodden and in
disrepair, be imprinted on your eternal memory.
Peer deeply into his moistened eyes and you will see your
spectacular miscarriage – normally afforded foe not flesh.

Belatedly the day has arrived
Tomorrow birds will sing like never before, young children will
play unfettered, and I will draw deep breathes of extrication
For you, perdition awaits – now your infinitude consort

# The Forever Field

Your presence aside, you did no wrong
Born to darkness to which there was no dawn
Inscrutable seclusion
She tried to protect you
Her soul no match for his reprehensible persecution
In arms, collateral damage, destruction that knows no end

Destruction that feasts off your fear
Devours your vulnerability
Your well of tears, lubricant for cogs of demise
I see you off in the distance
A young boy alone, face up in the forever field, having said
your silent goodbyes
Distance and time, no barrier to your pain

I embrace you
Your shivering body pervades mine for we are but one
Together we are whole
Your tiny hand in mind
We meander, picking up discarded fragments of your truth
A treasure trove of all that is pure

Together we garner what we can, our arms full as if gathering
firewood
Resigned to the reality that we have inevitably left behind

remnants
Remnants strewn far and wide that will lay idle enduringly but
for another day

# North

Born from serendipity
This friendship became
The product of migrants looking for land that they would one
day proclaim. North

Evolved from humble beginnings
Together battling demons to erase
All the while fanning each others ambitions
In search of new horizons to chase. North

One soul elevated by another
A precious life long gift
What have I done to deserve you?
Devastatingly set adrift – North

## Where is the Dawn?

They glare at you, susceptible by night – prostrate, frustrated,
desperately craving slumber.
That's when they are at their most assertive.
Fertile ground for your fears – fears having grown claws, anger
spawn teeth and darkest truths with hands each strong enough to
constrict your windpipe. Memories by day that offer hope and
warmth, now dragging you through an emotional quagmire
accentuating the ugly, the most painful…the stench of loss
Where is the dawn?…

## "Enough"

Enough of white noise and paralysing anxiety
Enough of insincere gestures and of the veiled villains to whom
they have become second nature
Enough of routine, of traffic that I once knew to be kinetic
Enough of my hapless Barista, Mario (may he part with his
business before my return)
Enough of gasping breaths and random sighs
Enough of gregarious hot air balloons that hover nonchalantly in
my morning sky as havoc permeates below
Enough of self judgement, doubt and disappointment
Enough!

## "Numb"

Numb at my fingertips
Decay at my toes
The pain of an orphan
So few of us know
A quiet moment
Or a moment too long
Finality by contemplation
Too fatigued to prolong
Existential crisis
Prognosis is dire
Too late to dissect?
So soon to expire

# The Warmth of The Sun

Whilst granting myself leave from the confinement of my office
and walking without intent, I looked down and momentarily found
solace in my shadow.
I closed my eyes and paid homage to the sun for acknowledging
my place, no matter how insignificant, in a world that sometimes
appears to be conspiring against me – today I needed as much…

# Almighty Pen

Aged seven, he recalled sitting desolate in the playground, preferring his own company to that of others.
His solitude ensured minimal "use" of his mangled vocal cords (as he had so diagnosed himself back then in lieu of a "costly" professional opinion), sparing him the ridicule of those ignorant to his plight.

They thought him lessor, perhaps even dim-witted, and often mocked him, unaware that his mind could construct commendably articulate sentences and further, deliver them effortlessly and with aplomb – albeit silently and to an attentive and sympathetic audience of one.

He often wondered why him. In what past wrong was he complicit to deserve such a curse? He often lamented what a heavenly existence it must it be to conceive of a sentence and represent it truly by way of spoken word.

It was no surprise then that his adolescence saw him drawn to the pen: a safe place where his ability to enunciate was limited only by the ink in his pen, the surface area of his notebook.
He would write for hours. Traversing thought after thought, making each sentence more descriptive than the last.
At times he would write with great fluidity and voraciousness

and at others he would become stagnant, stubbornly fastidious about the selection and use of his next word in contemplation of how it affected those that preceded and followed it – forever determined never to waste a phrase, a precious word.

As the chasm in our ages widens, I call on him with increased
frequency
An overly sensitive blonde boy with a stammer – his spirit at
odds with his grief
Sometimes it's adversity that engenders the most profound of
responses
Familiarity of pain that promotes relief

# D-D-D-D…

As he feels his throat dry and constrict, he apprehensively
reveals his aperture only to have primeval sounds stumble over
his tongue. Sounds intended to give life to flowery expression,
to capture emotion as experienced in real time. Instead, "words"
– words that get twisted, mutilated, rearranged and at times
abandoned like unwarranted children.

# Pass Me By

Some days are more agonising than others
Some days the sun doesn't shine
Some days there are no diversions
From which ones heart can hide
At times my soul feels raw
Feeling the full force of life's pain
Sometimes I sit in loathing
Of the place it all began
Somewhere there is a rainbow
Salvation in the sky?
No rainbows for the condemned
Colours pass me by

# The Larcenist

Sometimes the further you are
The closer they seem
The demons of your days, the terrors of your dreams
Distance can be deceiving – a larcenist in ways
Offering you calm
Before mischievously stealing it away…

# Death Masquerade

Demons cascading
Judgement degrading
Salvation blockading
Darkness pervading

Carnage you trade in
Land mines evading
Sunlight is fading
Death masquerading

# Subsistence

Life chipping away one thread at a time
What of the vow you made of an existence sublime?
Years as a child where carnage and terror would rein
Resisting the loneliness, the sadness and pain
What sense in reflection or bemoaning the past?
Subsistence in separation, spectators aghast...

# Ode to my iPod (Vintage Edition)

Heart felt gratitude;
For your unwavering companionship when night is day
For devouring the air miles
For distracting me from the inevitable waves of homesickness
For the gentle reminders of sorrows past
For nurturing my soul and for your insistence that without passion
and emotion, life is a fruitless journey

# Musical life crisis

I spent today dealing with what I have come to call my "musical life crisis". I first experienced it after seeing Elvis Costello in 1999 and now relapse whenever I encounter profound creativity. It leaves me sad, a little distressed and contemplative of my own humanity – wondering what I will leave behind when I'm no longer here...

# Forever Gone

The time between my Mum passing and her funeral were at best a blur. I recall feeling pain and not a lot else – I didn't really say a lot, nor did I pay a lot of attention to what others were saying. It was like I was dropped head first into an unrelenting state of grief and disbelief and for all intensive purposes I was paralysed. I was wondering just how I was going to get through the following day and the next, and the next...

It wasn't until after she had been laid to rest that, in retrospect, the long process of healing commenced.

After the funeral, I had a lot of problems dealing with how it seemed the world went about it's business as if nothing had happened, as if there was no cataclysmic event – the sun came up, fowl chirped, people got up and went to work in their cars – why? How dare they! – didn't they realise my mother had died and that the world would never be the same?!

After the first four weeks or so, I distinctly remember thinking that simply because I got up in the morning, had a shave and a shower, put on a suit and even managed a smile, people around me assumed that I was OK. I was not OK. I was hurting and on some level I wanted people to know it.

The first year was undoubtedly the hardest. All those

34

anniversaries, my birthday, her birthday, Easter, Xmas, her passing – all were agonising in there own way. Looking back, I now understand that they were very important milestones in my eventual emotional recovery. Some of these days are still difficult for me and at the very least are tainted with the loss of someone I loved with all my heart. I have resigned myself to understanding that on some level I will always feel this way, and that in itself is on some comfort.

So twenty years on and in many ways it's still painful to think of my mother – it's only the last few years that I've been able to attend others' funerals without mourning my mum. Thankfully, the periods between those moments of panging are getting longer and longer, as indeed they have since the first anniversary of her passing. Equally though, there are wondrous moments where my heart feels warm and full and I know my mum is close by, watching over me and my family. My girls, born after mum died, as toddlers would say that "Nanna sat on the end of our bed last night" – in my heart of hearts, I know this to be true.

She will forever be in my heart and she is safe and content there.

## Mixed Tape – Dedicated to the enomoirty of talent lost in 2016

Here today, gone tomorrow
All that's left is the songs we borrow
The anthems of our youth, the lyrics of lost love
The alchemists who scribe them
Now watch peacefully from above
Where do they go when they leave this earth?
Perhaps they ascend to paradise, their souls duly rested before rebirth?
Why does it matter? Why should we care?
To live without their music
Is to live in despair

# Where Are We Now?

I sat up in a hotel bed at two am, played his music, exhausted my mini bar of anything vaguely resembling whiskey and wept. I cried for David Bowie, I cried for David Jones, I cried for his family but mainly I cried for myself and the millions like me, left empty, mourning his finality.

I woke expecting the world to be a different place.
I felt reluctant, and somewhat vulnerable stepping outside for fear of exposing myself to grief on a mass scale.

As I walked down Geary St toward Union Square to my first meeting of the day, on what was a brisk winters San Francisco morning, I offered a look of empathy to those that walked past me. I was anticipating an outpouring of emotion, a profound sense of loss – but it wasn't forthcoming. People, it seemed, woke at their normal time that day, took their regular showers, got dressed and went off into the world as though it was a day like any other.
But he was gone, forever gone. He would never write another lyric, sing another song, wear another outrageous outfit.
Part of me felt envious of those that heard the birds chirp that day, felt the warmth of the intermittent sun and remained ignorant to the enormity of his passing.
It may not have been felt in everyone's heart, but the world did change that day and it will now never be the same. "Planet earth is {indeed} blue"

# An Ode to Marcus (and the World's special needs children)

I know I'm not like them
Or rather they are not like me
What they fail to understand is that
This is who I chose to be
God took me to one side
And uttered "for you there is a choice
You can join the dreaded masses
Or help the unsuspecting rejoice"
I may not be of learning
I may not be like you
But I am not caught up in material things
And of your frustrations, I have few
He sent me to teach you compassion
I've come to teach you truth
I have to come to help you mend your ways
Yet you mistake my time on earth for youth
So if I cross your path in life
Perhaps struggling with menial tasks
Spare a thought for those less fortunate
For its time to lose your mask

Trundling with ones head hung, summons darkness and fear
My love, my dearest one, gaze toward the heavens for they will
shower you with healing light and inner peace
Be still, expand the god given cavity that grants the breath that
serves to soothe even the most fractured of souls.

# Autumn

The last leaves of autumn, hang on in despair. The last leaves of autumn "let go if you dare". Your efforts are futile, the seasons dictate. Your eventual demise, your inevitable fate.

# Purpose

There is purpose in elation
Purpose in sorrow
Purpose in yesterday
Purpose in tomorrow
Purpose in indulgence
Purpose in going without
Veiled purpose in being agnostic
Purpose in being devout
Purpose in the daylight
And purpose in its shade
Purpose in indulging, in that which is forbade
Purpose in adversity
God forsaken purpose in pain
Purpose in not knowing, if we'll have that time again
Purpose in a shudder
Purpose in a breath
Purpose to the last
Purpose in our death…

# The Unwritten Letter

I woke one day, and she was gone.
I sat in silence beside her, my hand on hers. Tears rolling down my face, waiting for them to come. Secretly praying they would never.

Before I knew it, I was there alone.
Everything I looked at, every scent, every thought, painfully reminded me of her.
Suddenly it dawned on me. Maybe she had left behind a note. I searched feverishly, beginning in the bedroom and systemically working my way through our home trying my best to put things neatly back in their place – she hated how fastidious I could be.

For months, and on a whim my attention diverted, I would comb through another little nook of our home, now reduced to nothing more than bricks and mortar, in the hope I had missed a small envelope, perhaps tainted with her favourite perfume.

I can still remember the moment I conceded, lying prostrate on my couch, my head and heart aching in equal measure. I closed my eyes, wishing it would all end.
I felt myself thankfully slipping into slumber, my emotional state of surrender.

That's when she came to me. She sat on the ground beside me, silent, her hand on mine. Tears rolling down her face, waiting for me to wake. Secretly praying I would never…

# Daily Introspection

Fight or flight
From the depths of despair
Bruised and battered soul
In need of repair

Fight or flight
Does it know no bounds?
When all is said and done
Is there no peace to be found?

Fight or flight
Dreading the dawn
Another day in the battlefields
Enough! – curtains drawn

# A Gesture Unforseen – (Burden of the Wealthy)

If it's easier to judge me
If it's easier to deny
The substance of the man
That this life is by the bye

If it's easier to tell yourself
This path is so horribly wrong
Than to allow yourself to be there
Than to listen to my song

If it's easier to live your life
Judging me a lessor being
Then I'll wrap that up and gift it to you
A gesture unforeseen (?)

# The Cancerian

Finally an end to solitude, to soulless hotel rooms, to pretending
that night is day and day night; an end to distracting my wretched
heart from the inevitable pangs of homesickness and my head from
the dull ache of fatigue.
At last some reprieve from living out of a suitcase and confusing
one city for the previous. Good riddance to protracted airport
security queues and those that obsess about being first to board and
disembark an aircraft – even though I am among them.
Home is where this Cancerian is most content…

# Room For Five

Faced with yet another lonely night in a soulless hotel room, he bustles through the door and with urgency opens his suitcase on the first available flat surface, thereby unleashing four precious souls, each of which dutifully dance their way to respective corners of the ceiling – vantage from which they'll lovingly guide him through slumber, offering resilience and promoting dreams of soon being back in their embrace.

# FICTIONAL INTERLUDE

# An Italian Trilogy

## Positano – A Fable

The year was 1343. As he did every day the sea permitted, Salvatore woke at three am. Sitting alone at his table made from native wood, his pipe in one hand a coffee in the other, he tries to ignore the tiny price of bread remaining from the previous nights family meal accompanied only with olive oil. He lovingly refrains, putting his hunger to one side – a family man until the end.

As is his ritual he makes his way to his humble vessel and says a small prayer asking Poseidon, the god after which this poor impoverished fishing village of Positano was named after, for a prosperous mornings fishing.

Hour after hour his sits dutifully in the middle of the Mediterranean. Nothing. Not a bite nor nibble.

He wonders what his life could have been if he too left for Rome as a young man to become a stone mason as his elder brother Arturo did before him.

Not less than three and a half hours later the tension on his hand held line tightens. His heart beats through his chest. Finally some luck. For two hours he fought this fish – it was far bigger than his simple rig could handle. He looks down at his hands. Each bleeding from the sharpness of the fishing line. Slowly he wears the fish down. After a mammoth struggle he finally sees the silvery flesh rising to the surface. Just as he allows himself to bask in success his line breaks.

On his arrival back to the village his friend Francesco looks at him knowingly. He too knows that look of a down trodden fisherman.

Without even a word, Francesco helps secure Salvos boat and helps him onto the warf. Salvo falls into his friends arms weeping knowing his family will again go to bed hungry this evening. Francesco's fortune was better that morning. He reached into his basket, the base of which was coloured with four red mullet. He takes two of them and puts them in Salvatore's basket, barren no more.

Today some 800 years hence, the two friends sit quietly in a piazza in their heaven – a place where fresh fish is delivered to their doors every day at dawn. They look down on Positano with amusement – a place where people now flock from all over the world to bath, eat and drink.

They catch each others glance and smile, reflecting on their past hardships and the eternal friendship from which was spawn.

# Tree of Forgiveness

I'albero Del Perdono
(Inspired by our time in Anacapri)


Pierre Luigi lost everything in the fire. His humble home, his two daughters, his son and his beautiful childhood sweetheart, then wife, Vittoria who painstakingly bore his children – she was a tiny woman and these were simple times where births were natural regardless of consequence or risk.

In the midst of his unbearable grief he planted four lemon trees, – one each for those he lost.

Day after day he tendered lovingly to these trees regardless of weather. At dusk he would sit in his small orchard on a simple wooden stool he himself hand crafted and would speak to each tree referring to them by name, recalling loving memories and tender moments shared as he desperately wished he'd done before they were cruelly taken away.

After drinking sufficient wine to withstand the baring of his soul unleashing all the pain that encompassed it, he would cry and ask their forgiveness. If only he had been at home that day, rather than making the arduous journey into town to gather the months provisions, perhaps he could have saved them – or at the very least have been taken too, sparing him this tortured existence.

The years pass, still this solemn and gentle soul honours the promise he made to what were once saplings – he would not fail them again.

Seventy-three years of age now, his family gone for decades. His memories still vivid – the trees prosperous, baring large and sumptuous fruit season after season.

He sat and poured himself a particularly generous glass of wine that evening. He felt the wind pick up. It felt fresh and invigorating on his sun weathered face. Still the breeze got stronger – he found himself fretting for his family of trees. It may have been the wind whistling through the trees deceiving his ageing and feeble mind, but Pierre Luigi heard Vittoria whisper to give himself to the gale, as the trees seemed to do.

They found him ten days later lying beside his humble orchard, stool tipped over and an empty wine glass nearby.

His body was not embalmed – this was a ritual only afforded the wealthy. Rather he was buried simply at the sympathetic hand of a near by villager to whom the man was a stranger – Pierre Luigi a staunch recluse since losing his loved ones.

Many months later the same villager passing by on his donkey found himself drawn to the burial site. A man of god, he stood there poignantly saying a silent prayer for the anguished stranger at the mound of earth adjacent to the simple orchard of four lush lemon trees oblivious that a fifth tree had now begun to grow. It was nestled perfectly equidistant to the four mature trees, thereby providing it with the optimal protection and sun required to flourish. It was time for them to now nurture their devoted father and husband.

For now and forever after. As it was before.

# A Place for Good Men - Finale in this trilogy

Salvatore finished the last of his espresso, squeezed Francesco's hand in a show of friendship beyond that transcended words. Slowly making his way across the piazza he took in all his heaven had to offer: the bluest of skies, punctuated with white fluffy clouds each in the shape of fish. He walks as always at a leisurely pace humming the tune his mother would sing to him as an infant.

As he approaches his narrow street wonderfully lined with generous bergonias growing from each and every balcony that knew nothing of seasons, he catches the stare of a stranger. Somewhat fixated, he stops in his tracks.

The man gets up from the bench that he shares with his wife and three children – wonderfully decorated in porcelain tiles of blue, white and yellow that the proudest of lemon trees would boast.

He approaches Salvatore, his eyes welling up before each giving way to a stream of tears that traverse freely over his cheeks.

"Scusa mio caro amico (excuse me my dear friend), please forgive my tears. You don't know me but I you. In another lifetime you paid me the greatest of respects. Left to slowly rot in my orchard you dug a hole with your bare hands and laid my body to rest. Sometime later, from this very piazza, I saw you revisit my place of mortal rest. I heard your silent prayer asking that my soul should find peace and that I would find the ones dearest to me . Shortly thereafter, I was reunited with my family."

Pierre Luigi broke down and embraced Salvatore who later in life moved to Anacapri with his family in search of a life independent of the vagaries of the sea.

Salvatore was equally touched. He embraced Pierre Luigi with all the love and adoration one would show a brother. He walked Pierre Luigi back over to his family tucked safely under his arm, his wife Vitoria beaming with pride for the man she fell in love with as a fifteen year old. Pierre Luigi introduced each of them by name.

Salvatore gestured for them to follow him. Through the cobble stone street they followed him to his home where his wife had a prepared a feast of baked red mullet – now the fish of Salvatore's choosing, served only with fennel and the freshest of lemons. Together they broke bread and talked as if knowing each other forever as they now would in eternity.

Unremarkably these two devoted family men shared the same heaven. Why would they not?…

A final word:

It is with much sadness that I say farewell to Salvatore, Pierre Luigi and the women that stood loyally alongside each of them. I have shared their pain and rejoiced in their ultimate happiness.

At the time of writing "Tree of Forgiveness", I did not conceive of a trilogy nor that the obliging stranger should reveal himself as Salvatore. Perhaps he waited for my mind to drift sufficiently before gently prodding my subliminal, to suggest that which perhaps should have been obvious – to find a way to connect the two men knowing that whilst their stories were different, their morals were one in the same.

I'd like to think that somehow in an alternate universe they found each other – my role duly reduced simply to that of conduit.

Farewell miei cari amici

# A Place For Good Men - reprise

Many hundreds of years later, as futile as it seemed, Salvatore was unable to forget those mornings where an unexpected early sunrise would beat him back to the jetty, thus exposing his sometimes paltry catch to those hopeful villagers that littered Positano's molo (jetty).

He never imagined during his seventy-eight years that he would one day use his experiences, both painful and blissful, existentially to guide those that came after him.
To his surprise those heart wrenching moments at sea nurtured an inner strength that he would otherwise never possess, now in a place reserved for the good hearted, the honest and humble – irrespective of means.

Salvatore had come to honour his intuition, now a veritable art form he had crafted during the many hours he spent in silence each day watching over those of his blood that followed him on gods earth, many whom still boasted the emerald like eyes of his wife and only love Giuseppina.

Generation after generation he watched on, sometimes subtly nudging the subconscious of those still living out their mortal years.
He was protector, carer to those in need and confidant to those that dwelled in their minds, unaware that they were at times

conversing with someone that held them very dear.

The world had changed profoundly since his death, those of his blood now strewn overall corners of the earth. To the tiny Mediterranean island of Malta to an abundant colony since discovered by the British known as Australia.

One day as he gazed somewhat forlornly below, he himself felt a soothing hand on his shoulder.

The man, old and grey and also an elevated soul, felt the raw empathy Salvatore held for the one of his own struggling through life, who time and time again, resisted help from his ancestor high above.
"Hello Salvatore. Just as the thoughts of those below have summoned your heart, yours has mine. I am you're great great grandfather. I spent many mornings by your side on your humble barca da pesca (fishing boat) willing you on to persist, never lose hope and above all to hold your head up high – your integrity never in question."

Together, now hand in hand, they peered down at the middle aged man by the name of Carlo each feeling the crudeness of his angst, until Salvatore could bare it no more.
"Wait," said the elder of the two, "he is not yet ready to abandon his pain and accept his own forgiveness."
They waited patiently, for their descendants mind to wander toward a calmer place.

Sobbing, and questioning the abundance of tears in this seemingly bottomless well, Carlo silently asked himself, "How did I arrive at this desolate place in my life?"

At the same time, Salvatore's Elder squeezed his hand in a sign that the time was nigh.

Carlo took his hands from his eyes and looked with intrigue at the tear soaked creases that resembled scars in a form remarkably similar to those Salvatore bore from all those years of working with line and hook.

It was then that Carlo felt his emotional burden lift – albeit marginally.
The marks on his hands, as transient as they were, turned his mind toward the fight and tenacity that saw him desperately attempt to hold onto a life that was now in embers. Perhaps it was time to forgive himself, to relieve his guilt and shame, to become kinetic and whole once again.
He lent back into the nature that held him momentarily and gazed directly into the bluest of skies but not before catching a glimpse of a small orchard of lemon trees near by. He gave thanks for the glimmer of hope and strength bestowed upon him and made a silent promise to his angels that it would not be in haste – that this would be a small step forward that would serve to restore a once proud stride. He willed himself to persist, never lose hope and above all to hold his head up high – his integrity never in question.

Salvatore felt the fullness of breath return to his body, his hearts rest restored.

Every generation has its challenges, its fruitless endeavours at sea. From time to time, we must accept, if not embrace our "empty baskets" for they make those that are not seem more plentiful.

# Arancini (for Catia, a devotee)

At 3.3 km high and a circumference of some 140 km Etna, a stratovolcano, has stood proudly for over 500,000 years and is the largest of the three active volcanoes in Italy at two and a half times the size of Mount Vesuvius.

Greek Mythology suggests that the deadly monster Typhon was trapped under this mountain by none other than Zeus, the god of the sky and thunder and king of gods.

1287 was the last time Etna erupted to any significant degree. She caused fatalities that numbered in the thousands.

The day started with her gently releasing smoke from her vent as was more common than not these days.

The townsfolk of surrounding villages went about their daily duties – generations prospering from eruptions past that ultimately resulted in the most fertile of soil supporting vineyards and orchards of many varieties.

Later that day, a few tremors were felt beneath the feet of locals in the field. Whilst the younger ones thought little of it, those of more years looked up at her, sensing that perhaps this was no ordinary temper tantrum.

Within hours all hell broke lose, Etna now putting on a fireworks display that confirmed something more worrisome was afoot.

Suddenly her North Western side gave way and she began spewing in a exuberant show of life.

The villagers looked on in disbelief as there was no lava to be seen – only a river of mozzarella and sugo. Perhaps Hestia, Greek Goddess of all things domesticated, intervened.

Those that fled, stopped in their tracks before running toward her offering – some armed with pots others with loaves of bread. Those further afield flocked from Catania and Messina to partake in this culinary miracle.

That evening was one of celebration, if not glorification and five million Sicilians went to bed with bellies so full that they slept to noon the following day.

Each woke to a kitchen full of Etna's miracle stored in varied containers and stewing pots.

Faced with the inevitable task of putting it to good use, the arancini was born.

# HNY (for Carla)

Another year of elation, another year of tearful sorrow. Another
year of heart felt compassion, another year of impatience. Another
year of success, another year of failure. Another year to question,
another year to accept the inevitable. Another year of planning
meticulously, another year of inviting the wonderfully unexpected.
Another year to live, reflect, bathe in the company of those we love
and indulge in the breath...

# Today I wrote a list;

A list of things I WILL achieve in 2013…
A list of things I plan to tend to in the coming twelve months
A list of ambitions – a few of which I may get around to for filling
in their entirety during the course of the new year
An ambitious list of to-dos I'd love to see to in 2013 but in all
honestly, am unlikely to get around to…
All said and done I imagine I will spend the next year like every
other – trying to be the best husband, father, brother and friend I
can be – leaving the rest in the lap of the gods!
Today I threw away a list…

# Depression (inspired by Robin Williams)

Depression knows not the difference between rich and poor, famous and obscure. It is resolute in failing to discriminate between the groomed and filthy, the ambitious and the apathetic. Rather, it looms like a reaper threatening all of our lives, ready to take the unsuspecting away. If depression is the price to pay for 'progression' and commerce, then it is a price to high...

## 9/11 – A New Dawn

Today, on a short flight up to Tinsel Town (Sydney, Australia) I found myself anxiously contemplating the worst. What if that day saw a security guy on the take? What if technology had failed to do the requisite screening? What if there was a bomb on board? It could all be over in a breath, in a moment, without fuss or consciousness, surrounded not by people I love, but by strangers linked only by a flight number, a headline, an international incident.

# Fine Lines

I have always found there to be a point of enlightenment
experienced in the process of getting inebriated.
However brief, drinking delivers me momentary clarity of
thought and emotional insight into my inner being that I so
rarely experience sober. Alcohol, however evil, strips back my
inhibitions, magnifies my predispositions and gives me a candid
glimpse at my true self. Moments later, of course, I become an
asshole...

## Vasco Pyjama (based on the character of the same name created by Michael Luenig)

Vasco da Gama (1460- 1524) was a Portuguese explorer and significantly, was the first European to reach India by sea. In so doing he was responsible for the age of global imperialism and for the Portuguese to establish a long lasting colonial empire in Asia. Unopposed access to the Indian spice routes subsequently underwrote the Portuguese economy and political power for decades to come.

Like his name sake before him, Vasco Pyjama is an explorer but of a different kind, engrossed in his never ending and sometimes exhausting quest for truth and self-discovery – by his side is his ever faithful direction finding duck. Together they traverse the world, intermittently returning to Curly Flat to bath in the company of their long time friend and mentor Mr Curly, who unlike Vasco lives a very contented and still existence. There is much to learn from the dialogue between these two:

"It is worth doing nothing and it is worth having a rest. In spite of all the difficulty it may cause, you must rest Vasco – otherwise you will become restless."

In truth the world needs Vasco's of both kinds – those that go in search of commerce and new frontiers and those that strive for peace and contentment.

# Escape

Resent me for my sorrow
Detest me for my pain
Judge me for my innocence
Love knows not refrain

Despise me for my achievements
Mock me when I'm weak
Mistreat the one I'm most like
Escape is not defeat

# Blessed Be the Man

I've come to understand that an important measure of a mans life is the women he share's it with. Blessed am I that has:
A wife that is the most loving, warm and selfless person I know, embraces the good and bad in me in equal measure, and is there for our family unconditionally. I am a better person for being married to her;
A best friend that has helped nurture a once in (many) a life time friendship that remains a wonderful constant in a world full of uncertainty, malice and judgement;
An amazing mother in law that each and every day unknowingly helps ease the pain of losing my mother so early in my adult life;
And last but not least, a mother who left this earth twenty years ago to the day but continues to find ways of gently reminding me of her unrelenting love and oversight. My kids will grow up knowing exactly who you were. I love you with every fibre of my being, Mum. Xx
Blessed is the man…

# Mother Love

"A mother gives birth to you twice. Once when your born and once when she dies" – unknown

The more I reflect on this quote the more it resonates. Whilst birth is factual and beyond debate, I've sat with the later to make my own peace with my mothers death.
At face value and in the midst of what I can only describe as insufferable grief, the loss of my mother brought with it no immediate sense of rebirth. On the contrary, I felt the antithesis of birth in its rawest form. "How do I move forward from here?"
Now twenty years since mums passing, whilst I still struggle with the terrible injustice of Mum leaving us at only fifty-nine years of age, I have a better understanding of my so called rebirth. Whilst gradual, with grief and loss comes incredible growth – of empathy, strength of spirit, and an evergreen opportunity to live out your live with as much humanity as you can muster.

## Unlucky For Some

13 years of pain, 13 years of sorrow
13 years of knowing, there are to be no more tomorrow's
13 years to ponder what it could have…should have been like, for
you to know our children, for you to share their lives
13 years to savour the time we had together, 4,745 days to cherish
memories, held in our hearts forever
Miss you, Mum x

# Happy Mothers Day

Where to start for someone that has given you life?
That always put herself second, no sixth, for the sake of her boys
That embraced her role as grandmother as lovingly and with the
same dedication as she did mother
That loved to laugh and share in the excitement of those around
her
Where to start...?

# She (for Claudia)

She smiles when's she's happy
She smiles when she's sad
She smiles in the face of adversity
She smiles when she's glad
She smiles when she's hungry
She's smiles when she's tired
But she smiles the most for others
Her love and joy conspired

## Intermittent Interludes

Some people come to us as inadvertently, others caught in our wake.
Some stay intermittently, as if loitering on a street corner until something better presents, some resilient to the end.
Some have profound consequence, altering our course, others play cameos; all are of significance in this way or that.
Some people we don't mean to lose:
They snare in bear traps; they get lost in piazzas.
Some leave desolate voids, most of us resigned to live out our lives evading the inevitable scaring, others are quickly supplanted without aforethought, effect or repercussion.
Love and loss are fate filled, without which our lives rudderless, aimless and without purpose.

## Death in D.C.

As he trundled around this distant and unfamiliar city in a vain attempt to squander an afternoon, he noticed growing momentum whenever he turned a corner west ward – home and heart drawing him forth.

# Mile High

Suspended at 30,000 feet, and bathed in what at least momentarily would seem to be the perfect metabolic cocktail of fatigue, homesickness, and hunger – exacerbated perhaps by the cabin pressure that dances flirtingly with my temporal lobe, I feel my soul in all it's abundance rush outwards from it's sanctuary, my heart, toward the skin the keeps me whole. My hands and fingers tingle with the excitement of simply being, and I smile deeply and knowingly in appreciation of the very special people that grace my world. Sometimes a moment is all that is required to restore faith, to replenish barren and depleted wells, to discover one's next wind

# Rebirth

From one's ebb, there is no light – days come and go, darkness
pervades.
Such a predicament has ones soul yearning for willing and
forgiving shoulders that collectively establish a formidable
platform of pure love – vantage from which one might garner a
glimmer of brightness and warmth, a base from which the slow
process of rebirth can begin

Give yourself to the ocean for it awaits to cleanse your soul
Give yourself to the sun for it beckons to warm your heart
Give yourself to the wind – it will guide you along your path
Give yourself to pain for it is the source of your ultimate joy
Give yourself to those that love you most for they are
irreplaceable

# COVID by Sunrise

Today I woke early
I crept downstairs so as not to disturb anyone.
I made myself a hot beverage and sat idly at my desk.
I gave thanks for my family.
I gave thanks for my blessed friends.
I contemplated this horrendous turn of events and prayed
silently for those I love and for those that they in turn adore.
As I watched the sunrise I was overcome with a sense of hope. I
drew great strength from those that share my world, knowing
that one way or another we'll make it through this together.

# Me, Myself and Try

And in a moment of self doubt and vulnerability
I closed my eyes and suddenly found myself in your embrace
I gently put my head on your shoulder
And wept with sweet relief

As I stood there, wrapped in your loving arms
I felt my heart beat align with yours
I felt the warmth of your breath
I felt your reassuring presence in abundance

You whispered that I would be fine – that I was loved despite
my imperfections, failings and misjudgements,
That this journey was far from futile

I slowly opened my eyes and with renewed clarity and faith, I
thanked myself for what was a timely display of unwavering
support and compassion

## As It Was Before

He peered into her moistened eyes – her veil no more.
She clutched at his wounded soul.
His heart swollen, radiated – her's reciprocating without
hesitation.
Together they sat idled, embracing as if for dear life.
As one they are resilient.
For now and ever after.
As it was before.

## Four - a tribute to the victims of Australia's devastating bush fires

She woke as she had for each of the last four days – with a heavy heart, head in hands.

Her last conscious thought before finally falling into slumber only a few hours prior, a simple pray that this obliteration a terrible dream – again gone unheard. Where was her god? she angrily queried.

With hands drenched, salted discharge from her eyes – eyes with seemingly endless wells of tears, she forces herself through what is now her early morning ritual, committing to memory the four most precious things lost to fire. She forces the recollection of intricate details – irreplaceable and now scattered in embers over an unquantifiable land mass.

As she acknowledges the last – an audio recording of her four children as infants singing, "happy birthday, Mum," hearing each voice as if unaccompanied, she draws on all of her inner strength to lift her head, drying her hands on her tear-stained t-shirt.

She squints and resists the pain of the morning sky – grey and smoke filled but still punctuated with beams of strong light, the sun doing its god given best to replenish those in need.

She looks to her left and right scanning for familiarity amongst the four thousand or so that too have found refuge in the foreshore.

She draws strength from faces, faces that could be her own, yet somehow each uniquely distinguished by an amalgam of smoke,

83

grief and sleeplessness.

She turns and peers out toward the water, elated by the naval vessel some four kilometres offshore – salvation for her and her two remaining children. Elation is rudely supplanted by the constriction of her throat as she now faces the inevitable – the dread of leaving behind those lost forever.

In her heart, forever four.

## Sweet Oblivion

And under a mushroom in the corner of my garden, in the corner of the universe, a tiny but vibrant ecosystem continues along its merry way oblivious to the heart ache and hardship being felt across the globe. Just another day at 'Shroom HQ.

# The Hugger (for Aunty Chris)

I'll forever be grateful for the day you showed up on my
doorstep after we lost Mum, just to give me a hug – we had
never hugged before.
"I never really hugged my sister despite loving her with all my
heart. I'm not letting that happen again," you said holding me
tightly with all the love and compassion of a mother.
After that, we hugged every time we saw each other, until you
too suddenly passed. I've been a hugger ever since, in part in
the hope you're watching on.

Alone with myself
Save for the moon
Alone with my thoughts,
Best intentions impugn

She was an open book
He was illiterate
– a love story for the ages

# Harvest

We each sat there in silence
Acknowledging the
Others' pain
Vowing to one other
We won't go through this again

Bound by love and torment
No need for futile words
Our eyes yet again moistened
Speak of terror, a future blurred

Then one day she departed
Now in battle on my own
Until she whispered from afar, "It's time to take your leave my
love
Be sure to take seeds we have sown."

## 'Orphan'

I yearned simply as a child yearns
I reached out but instead you raised your hand
I craved tenderness – you offered hostility
We dare not bow to your demands

I bled because you cut me
I'm left disfigured because you failed
I am orphaned because you made her leave
She's gone – her soul prevails

# The Summer Home

The summer home sits dormant for months at a time.
No one there to acknowledge it's creaks and melancholic sighs.

From time to time it gently weeps, ultimately finding solace in
summers past.

As the weather turns late in the calender year, the summer home
idles in nervous anticipation. It's mood shifts, gradually but
with increasing momentum.

Soon thereafter the summer home draws on all its strength
(preserved for precisely this purpose), to lift its spirits ahead of
the imminent arrival of those it holds dearest.
It tries to breathe but is somewhat constricted by doors and
windows clenched. Nevertheless, modest success.

Cometh the day they finally arrive, the summer home can
hardly contain its excitement, now providing the energy
commensurate with those of its inhabitants.
So respectful is the summer home that it regulates its
exuberance, mindful of the need of others to regenerate and rest
in the first instance.
The summer home is sometimes forlorn but always patient in
acknowledgment of the mutual love and respect now
demonstrated over many years.
It's happiest when full of love and life, feeding exponentially
off the families that grace it.

# #metoo

For every dirtbag, there is a loving husband
For every sleeze, a devoted father
For every misogynist, a humanitarian
Don't condemn us all.

# Subsistence

Reliving the past, one car crash at a time
What of the vow you made to us all of an existence sublime?
Years as a child where fear and terror would rein
Resisting the loneliness, the sadness and pain
What sense in reflection or bemoaning the past?
Subsistence in separation, spectators aghast…

# Calm Before We're Called

Longing to remember what I once tried in earnest to forget.
Insisted on moving forward without dealing with regret.

Looking only toward the future – never looking back.
Repression is a cancer just waiting to attack.

Temporarily healing wounds, perhaps forgoing a chance to
grow.
Convinced I had beaten those demons – how was I to know?

With age we find resilience, the will and grace to face it all.
A chance to make our peace, be calm before we're called…

# Dinner For Two

He arrives at the same time every second Tuesday.

He insists on the same table by the front window (we dare not give it away) where at dusk the light is soft and playful. Despite this his eyes look perennially glassy yet worn.

He orders the very same bottle of wine, drinking all but enough to fill one last glass which he pours out opposite him, topping himself up if by chance he has miscalculated and there is residual.

He stares aimlessly into the street as if waiting for someone to cross the busy road, kiss him knowingly on the cheek, sit down and chat about his thoughts, ideas and dreams.

But no one ever comes. How could she…?

# Nom de Plume

Opaque at times, others translucent no end
Leaving some to ponder, others impugn
"Surely he speaks in the third person? Perhaps not...
This man, this tortured Nom de plume"

His pain, his angst, the heaviness of his heart
Familiarity in his turn of phrase – his perennial desire to swoon
Perhaps I know him, this tormented soul,
This man, this Nom de plume

I should have heard his cries of help
The sincerity of his plea
A clustering of words subliminally strewn
Now I sit listening to others recite him
Lost to the forever field, no longer Nom de plume

North, West, South, East
One road the light
One road the beast…

## The Larcenist

Sometimes the further you are
The closer they seem
The demons of your days, the terrors of your dreams

Distance can be deceiving – a larcenist in ways
Offering you solitude
Before mischievously stealing it away…

# New Years Revolution

Another year of elation, another year of tearful sorrow. Another year of heart felt compassion, another year of impatience.
Another year of success, another year of failure. Another year to question, another year to accept the inevitable. Another year of planning meticulously, another year of inviting the wonderfully unexpected.
Another year to live, reflect, bathe in the company of those we love and indulge in the breath…

# A One in A Hundred Year Tale

I'd like to dedicate this piece to all those who through Covid
have had to depart in the worst way possible and the hospital
staff that offered some solace. X

A man of eighty-three years I have lived a true life, a sincere
life.
As I lie here in intensive care, I desperately try to recall my
years, wondering what I may have done to deserve this end, this
desolation.
I'm alone with only my thoughts, my ponderance and the
wretched humming of the ventilator placed above my head and
to the right.
Thirteen days now of chronicling my past. My childhood where
I plodded through life in the northern suburbs of Melbourne
without intent or burden, my adolescence when my heart was
torn apart by the death of my mother, and my later life filled
with tender and loving moments surrounded by my children
spawned from love, the unsurpassable love of my life.
Time seems to pass languidly and yet time is all I crave. Time
to embrace my loved ones just once more, time to feel a
Melbourne winters breeze on my face, time to tell my dearest
consort that she is my world and without her I am lessor. Time
to beg forgiveness for those I may have wronged, time to make
peace with my journey.
I can feel myself gradually slipping away, my soul preparing to

liberate itself from my aging body.

As I take my final breathes, there is a tireless nurse at my side. She looks at me with empathy, holding my hand tightly in a final gesture – her grasp a potent conduit for the abundance of love from those nearest and dearest. In the distance I hear my mother's tender voice, "It's OK, my darling. I'm here and waiting for you with open arms…"

Trundling with one's head hung summons darkness and fear
My love, my dearest one, gaze toward the heavens for they will
shower you with healing light and inner peace
Be still, expand the god given cavity that grants the breath's
passage to soothe even the most impaired of souls

# Five Lil' Sparrows

Of late I have woken early to honour a recurring rendezvous
with a family of five little sparrows that have taken to gracing a
late autumn's tree in the yard behind my humble home – barren
if not for those little feathered creatures of gods making.

I sit there waiting – coffee in hand. Despondent that I may have
been stood up. Not today!!
On approach they flutter frantically, in majestic chaos before
each settling on their distinct branch – distant enough to flirt
with a sense of independence, yet close enough to intuitively
sense security in their joint sanctity.
Suddenly, and for no apparent reason one of the sparrows falls
to the ground – lying on its side, its unincumbered wing
scuffling as if to signal its impairment to the others.
I got up from my seat, my impulse to go to the sparrows aid.
I sat back down and watched as nature took its course.
Three of the remaining sparrows instantly make their way to the
base of the tree. The last remained at its post – head moving
feverishly, now scouting for any would be predators.

The larger of the three now grounded birds, wedged itself
between the ground and the injured bird. The other two fell
dutifully into place, the first positioning itself directly under the
uninjured wing, the other hopping and gently prodding from the
rear.

Together they slowly disappeared into the safety of the shrubbery – it was only then that the designated sentinel joined the others, perhaps relieved that its duties did not extend beyond its frantic surveying.

I was left pondering whether the bird in need of salvation was a parent or that of offspring. Had the inevitable cross over point in life where the young becomes primary caretaker already been breached?

Consumed in that thought for another moment or so, I realised it mattered not who was extricated, nor who nurtured who.

Unfettered love transcends species and ages of all kinds, parents and their young alike and at one time or another we all need a helping hand.

# Four Lil' Sparrows – chapter 2/Gods Speed

Winter approached rapidly – all fowl sensed its pending onset
and were equally perturbed by the chill in the air, an indication
of challenging times ahead.
He didn't want to leave his four little sparrows, yet in his tiny
heart of hearts he conceded forlornly that this was not a matter
requiring discretion. His endeavour to provide for his family,
dwarfing all that was familiar, all that was safe.

He set off Northward, turning his ponderance to all he holds
near and dear.
He reflected on tragedies past – for it was all too recent that he
fell from his perch, only to be sheltered and protected by those
he loved most, until he recovered to resume his paternal role
with the rigour and determination to which his family were
accustomed.

Sometimes even the sturdiest of nests are compromised and
sometimes selflessness is fortitude.
Gods speed, my friend. Gods speed. X

Today I dare not put pen to paper – terrified of giving life to my inner most thoughts

Some days just tears. Just loneliness. Just defeat in its most heart wrenching form.

# The Humble Peasant

She left nothing but a short note with the strictest of instructions, to be read as soon as was practicable upon her passing.

As it turned out, seventeen surrounded her bed as she took her final shallow, yet somewhat satisfying breath.

Her eldest daughter charged with the aforementioned request read out the following:

"My dear family – those of my blood, others that have nourished it. I bless each of you and wish you well on your extant journey. Entrust that I'll remain ably by your side, just as those already gone have held me in times of need.

Always remember that in life there is joy and hardship, both are of importance in nurturing an abundant soul. Understand that there is no clear delineation between pain and exuberance as it may portend in a still photograph.

I've included such an image of me as a young impoverished young girl, as joyful as one could imagine, buoyed in the moment only by the prospect of collecting our weekly ration of bread and milk.

Each of you know my story of so called prosperity. I was married to a man of means and lived my adult life surrounded by material possessions abound.

Whilst there were wonderful times shared, I often drew strength from this young girl, full of momentary glee and gratefulness that somehow went astray in an adult life mostly unfulfilled.

Treasure good and bad as you traverse through life, for both engender kind and meaningful souls that foster the most powerful of ripple effects of compassion and such, for future generations to build on."

# Ode to Izzy

Together we sat, paw in hand
There is so much I want to say to you, yet somehow my
tortured reflection in your eyes makes that redundant

As I would lead you on your morning walks, you led me from
one safe place to the next – at times helping me traverse the non
traversal (of note the sometimes wrenching artery from couch to
bed carefully guiding me past the perilous three empty
bedrooms toward our sanctuary of sweet slumber.)

In my darkest moments you would appear next to me, your head
resting gently on the vacant pillow next to me.

Forever and ever true confidant x

# The Passageway

Each night he trundles down the desolate hallway toward his
master bedroom – a place of sanctuary without doubt, but an
excruciating journey none the less peppered with memories of
better times.
Passing their doors one by one, behind which a sea of emptiness
idles, he says a silent good night to each of them, accompanied
with an I love you, I miss you.

The morning following, he wrestles with his bed ware, willing
himself back to sleep – to little avail.
He understands the inevitability of confronting the passageway
that he left behind with solace only a handful of hours ago.
He opens his bedroom door, resisting the temptation to slam it
shut and retreat.
He walks hesitantly the length of home met only with deafening
silence at every juncture.
He holds his head in his hands, as has become his custom, turns
around and retraces his steps with haste to where his moistened
pillow again awaits offering sanctity.

# Crevasses

We live in parallel with an ethereal world, a plethora of potholes, crevasses and chasms occupied by the injured, the maimed, the tortured. We are here not by chance, nor are we scattered haphazardly – in this way or that we are all connected, paths woven by ill-fated destiny, veiled by varied and convoluted degrees of separation.

When you happen upon us, peer deeply. Reach blindly for downtrodden souls that flicker rather than radiate, whimper not roar, fade rather than burgeon.

For we crave solitude, yet salvation; finality, yet hope; to be mourned, yet to be rejoiced.

# Death Wish

If I am to leave,
I leave on my feet.
Wearing my favourite shoes
And my best smile.
Upright, hands in the air
Dancing to my favourite tune
Surrounded by those I love the most.

# Le Chemin périphérique (fiction)

(The Peripheral Path)

Virginie Bracquemond moved haphazardly through her adult life. The youngest daughter of Benoit, a humble fromager who prided himself in proffering Parisian cheesemongers the best product he and his two eldest daughters could muster.
You see unlike her siblings, Virginie in no way inherited her father's love, nor discernment for cheese.

Hour after hour Benoit would patiently sit with his youngest, her eyes closed shut before he would unveil a procession of cheeses under her nose. "Take your time, my little one, tell me what variety of cheese you smell." To no avail, time and time again Benois sat patiently with Virginie urging her to "contemplate beyond the initial and most obvious fragrance, to experience the full effect of the cheese's bouquet, it's body, it's mystique – it's artistry."
She wanted only for her father's affection and prayed each night that she would wake with the same gift her sisters seemed indiscriminately bestowed.

No mater how she tried, Virginie could not differentiate between one and the next – nor did she have the heart to tell her father she found the smell rather repugnant.

Virginie, a common female name of the early 1800s and the name of her paternal grandmother, watched on well into her adolescence as her sisters worked feverishly with their father, leaving her feeling somewhat unworthy and detached from Benoit's love. For her peace of mind, Virginie assured herself that the day would come for them to catch up on time forfeited and form a father-daughter bond for the ages. Her dream came to an abrupt end however, when Benoit was abruptly taken by diphtheria only days before her seventeenth birthday.

Virginie, now fatherless and heartbroken, took to painting, where she would fleetingly find peace in her distraction. Somewhat ironically, she was drawn to the rather pervasive smell of her oil paints and from time to time even got lost in a subtle state of delirium – Virginie found this to be conducive to the creative process.

With time, she relished taking to a blank canvas to express a nuanced thought or ponderance or to express her inner most feelings. Virginie, herself was often surprised by the twists, twinning and implications resulting from an incremental stroke of her brush, more often than not the result of surrendering to the subconscious.

Now a "vieille fille" (spinster) in her early 40s, every Sunday, together with her paintings astride a trolly her father made for her as a child, now with retro fitted twine strong enough to secure her compositions, Virginie ventured to the nearby country town of Chartres, to take her place in the most west facing position in the local market.

She was not one for commerce, hoping only to sell enough

paintings to pay for her next batch of canvasses and replenish her paints – no more and no less, for they were her children.

By this measure, her time at market could come to an abrupt end once she had filled her quota – packed up and on her way within minutes. Other days she was seen to be sitting there alone until dusk desiring an incremental sale that never came.

Her "work" typically sold within three months of completion. The one exception was that nearest and dearest her heart – now eight years old with little ever buyers interest. She put this down to ignorance rather than substance.

The first Sunday after All Saints Day, Virgine made her way to the market as usual despite a torrid nights sleep in high winds.

Customers were sparse that day, so she sat directly in the sun, hoping its warmth would make the day, and her trip home more manageable.

She gave herself to slumber only to be woken moments later by a gentle hand on her shoulder.

She slowly opened her eyes and saw before her the feet of a middle aged man. She looked up, the sun accentuating his silhouette and leaving his face in darkness.

"That painting, my dear," he said pointing to Virginie's favourite work. "It is exquisite in its subtlety. It speaks of love, of loss and discontent – but also of something incomplete." It was then that Virginie realised it was Benois, her father – she would recognise that voice anywhere. With that, her father sat beside her and together they had the conversation she dreamed of having in another life time, and concurrently had the epiphany that this void was the source of the "discontent and "incompleteness"

Benois saw in Virginie's favourite piece.

Virginie sat and listened to her father as he told her she was always his favourite. "All that time, you were listening, weren't you, my little one? Once I had left, I guided you toward your own path to the periphery, you used it masterfully to inform that which is prominent – flirting with the abstract to further define that which is in focus. In my mortal years I did this with cheese, you have done the same in your wonderfully informed paintings."
With that, Benois squeezed his daughter's hand warmly and was gone.
Virginie was jolted back into her reality, quickly collected her belongings and headed home with the fullest of hearts – something not experienced in her many years.

With real intent Virginie sat before her easel with her favourite painting mounted, poured herself a glass of red wine and devoured a slice of Vieux boulonge (the most fragrant of all French cheeses) that she had impulsively bought on the way home.
She stills her conscious mind like never before waiting for the inevitable – a succession of strokes, perhaps guided by Benois, that transforms what was once in part a solemn work into something wondrous, now suspended by a young girl's perpetual love for her father.

# Vamos Despacio (fiction)

Don Diego de Espinosa sat solemnly astride the bow of the newly christened "Vamos Despacio". Traditionally, prominent sailors of yesteryear believed that the name of a ship helped bring good fortune and safety to the vessel, it's crew and passengers, whilst also allowing it to prosper in the manner for which it was built.
The Vamos Despacio, initially named The Todo Conquistando, was a grand Galleon fabricated to help dominate the great sea of thieves. Instead she now daundered without real intent toward Cadiz, where the Mediterranean flirts with the Atlantic.

Unlike his great grandfather, the great conquistador Herman Cortés (who established strong holds in the Central America's and Caribbean's in the early 1500s), Don Diego had no such aspirations, preferring instead to surrender to the bidding of the seas currents than chart a well defined course.

Vamos' centre of gravity was dictated not by the calculated placement of a bounty of great treasure won at battle, but by the pliancy of tears that occupied her bulge, accumulated over Don Diego's many "aimless" and desolate voyages.
As he sat and contemplated the horizon, he was overcome by the relief that accompanied the thought of bequeathing himself, in perpetuity, to the sea – a more forgiving fate than facing constant comparison to his younger, yet more revered and accomplished brother, The Admiral Don Miguel de Espinosa.

Contemplating his demise, Don Diego gave way to free flowing tears – veritable salt to the sea. He shed tears for his lost mother with whom he shared the softest of hearts, tears for his love now won by another, tears for his failure to live up to the incessant expectations of his steely father and his ancestors that preceded him.

As Don Diego wept, the undercarriage below, now overcome with tears, began to compromise the vessel's buoyancy. She heaved menacingly from left to right, her sole passenger as kinetic as the water below him, until she inevitably capsized.
Don Diego now at one with the sea, again with his dear mother and bound to his "mistress", The Vamos Despacio, now destined forever to "Go Slow".

# Feet of Clay

My Love is perfect but for feet of clay – fine grained malleable earth that can be moulded when wet. When dried, clay is used to cultivate things of treasured beauty such as pottery and ceramics, or alternately with more utility in forming foundations on which to construct wonderful mezzanines, gables and turrets.

At his most vulnerable, my Love's tears morph clay into mud, yet he still stands a foot above his rivals with absolute humility and aplomb – a soul to be admired.
Better feet of clay than a heart of stone.

## The Empty Heart

Some hearts recall lobster pots – hollow and cold – flailing in a
seemingly fathomless sea.
Due to extreme porosity, some pots are doomed for failure, with
openings and chambers exacerbated by too many years at sea.
Despite best efforts, all manner of vermin and treasure come
and go haphazardly without ramification, save the empty heart.

# He Writes

He writes because he needs to
To rid himself of pain
He writes to protect his heart
To defend his sun from rain

He writes with rigour in desperation
To express his thoughts concise
He writes because he failed him
In favour of wealth – his son's dignity sacrificed

He writes because he lost her
To let her know she is missed
He writes for fear of losing her
To keep her in his midst

He writes to provide direction
Guided by his heart
He writes as a poet might
To mend his soul, apart

Some days just tears.
Just loneliness.
Just defeat in its most heart wrenching form

# Authenticity

The authenticity of torment
Without which we know no exuberance

The validity of finality
Without which there are no new beginnings

The truth of solitude
Without which there is no endearment

The legitimacy of death
Without which there can be no life

# My Idol - A Banbury Story

My idol wears dilapidated commoners boots.
Extremities shackled by fate – dragging of limbs.
I look down forlornly at my delicate slippers delivered by the
master shoe maker himself only the evening before.
eighteenth century London, such was class divide.

Each morn at the break of dawn I watched, poised on the velvet
cushioned alcove of my bedroom bay window, as affliction did
it's darnedest to shatter a human spirit – my Idol hardened to the
core.
Unrelenting, she maneuverered with an elevated sense of
purpose, disappearing around the nearest corner as quickly as she
appeared – such were our daily 'interludes'.

In my mind, I would concoct Banbury stories, fictionalising the
rest of her day. Perhaps she worked at the royal palace at the
beckoning of the young princess. Perhaps she was making her
way to the theatre district in costume befitting her character.
Perhaps she was indeed a pauper, who went in search of scraps
for her thirteen children!

One day whilst playing hide-and-go-seek with Timothy, my
younger brother, I rushed into the servants kitchen basement
where I came face to face with my Idol "Hitty" on hands and
knees scouring the kitchen floor with an instrument of almost

toothbrush proportions. She laboured across the stone floor fastidiously removing any and all marks, presumably for little more than fiddlers pay.

Uncharacteristically, mother showed her face and referred to my Idol only as "you antiquated rogue" and proceeded to berate and ridicule her until her eyes welled up. Without knowing what she was apologising for, Hitty replied, "Yes, ma'am. It won't happen again, ma'am." The stench of embarrassment and shame will never leave me.

My Idol is "little more" than a Scullery Maid, assistant herself to the Kitchen Maid. A widow of four children, she sought no aide, too proud to put her case to the "local charitable overseers".

My Idol petitioned no pity, despite being the lowest ranked of all servants – not permitted to eat at the communal servants' dining table.

She cared unequivocally for the welfare of her offspring, who relied on her getting through another torturous day, indirectly at the hands of my wretched mother. Hitty's brood were not spared the reality that two in five families of the time lived below the 'breadline' – in no small part due to elevated grain prices. Such was my Idol's compassion, that once her children were fed, she would dutifully package and serve up any residual to her neighbour, an old spinster of little to no means.

At odds with my Idol, the woman who gave birth to me was teeming with superficiality and forever confusing shared biology with a true mother-daughter relationship – Hitty, a mother in every sense of the word.

My mother born to money, contaminated by the same. She had little to offer the world but barbarianism. She thought nothing of philanthropy, instead wearing her good fortune like a tiara of pretentiousness.

My mother socialised only with nobility, thumbing her nose at the gentry and the aristocracy who, despite their wealth, held no formal title. Her days were mostly filled with sauntering from one social occasion to the next in the finest of Chopines, a fine platform shoe of the day made from Europes finest silk – her feet as subtle as the day she was born. Yet another abhorrent display of pomposity.

My Idol wears dilapidated commoners boots.

This morning as our paths crossed intermittently and somewhat serendipitously, you were justifiably oblivious to the great strength I drew from the familiarity of your smile, my heart a-gush.

# Without

A life without pain
Is a life incomplete

A life without pain
Leaves a soul devoid of resilience

A life without pain
Is a life filled with complacency

"Hello" and "goodbye" are but wondrous parenthesis – the significance of which informed by the utter exuberance of the former, the heart breaking agony of the later